Alice Wong

easterseals

CHERRY LAKE PRESS

Published in the United States of America by Cherry Lake Publishing Group
Ann Arbor, Michigan
www.cherrylakepublishing.com

Reading Adviser: Beth Walker Gambro, MS, Ed., Reading Consultant, Yorkville, IL
Book Designer: Jennifer Wahi
Illustrator: Jeff Bane

Photo Credits: © Sean Pavone/Shutterstock, 5; © poo/Shutterstock, 7; © ChiccoDodiFC/Shutterstock, 9; © Susan Merrell/UCSF, 11; © 360b/Shutterstock, 13; The White House via Wikimedia Commons (CC BY 2.0), 15; © belushi/Shutterstock, 17, 22; © Scott Strazzante/San Francisco Chronicle/Polaris, 19, 23; © alia Herman/Guardian/eyevine/Redux, 21

Cherry Lake Press is an imprint of Cherry Lake Publishing Group.

Library of Congress Cataloging-in-Publication Data

Names: Hawley, Erin, author. | Bane, Jeff, 1957- illustrator.
Title: Alice Wong / written by Erin Hawley ; illustrated by Jeff Bane.
Description: Ann Arbor, Michigan : Cherry Lake Publishing, [2023] | Series: My itty-bitty bio | Audience: Grades K-1 | Summary: "Be proud. Be seen. Writer and organizer Alice Wong's life and legacy is explored in this biography for early readers. Her work for disability representation and accessibility is presented in a simple, age-appropriate way that helps young readers develop word recognition and reading skills. Developed in partnership with Easterseals and written by a member of the disability community, this title helps all readers learn from those who make a difference in our world. The My Itty-Bitty Bio series celebrates diversity, inclusion, and the values that readers of all ages can aspire to"-- Provided by publisher.
Identifiers: LCCN 2023009116 | ISBN 9781668927304 (hardcover) | ISBN 9781668928356 (paperback) | ISBN 9781668929827 (ebook) | ISBN 9781668931301 (pdf)
Subjects: LCSH: Wong, Alice, 1974- | People with disabilities--United States--Biography--Juvenile literature. | People with disabilities--United States--Social conditions--Juvenile literature.
Classification: LCC HV1552.3 .H39 2023 | DDC 305.9/08092273--dc23/eng/20230417
LC record available at https://lccn.loc.gov/2023009116

Printed in the United States of America
Corporate Graphics

About the author: Erin Hawley is disabled, nerdy, and wordy. She is a book lover, passionate gamer, and proud Latina. When she is not writing, she works as an accessibility consultant. She helps make games fun for everyone.

About the illustrator: Jeff Bane and his two business partners own a studio along the American River in Folsom, California, home of the 1849 Gold Rush. When Jeff's not sketching or illustrating for clients, he's either swimming or kayaking in the river to relax.

About our partnership: This title was developed in partnership with Easterseals to support its mission of empowering people with disabilities. Through their national network of affiliates, Easterseals provides essential services and on-the-ground supports to more than 1.5 million people each year.

I was born in Indiana. I am Asian American.

Where do you live?

I have a **disability**. My body gets weaker.

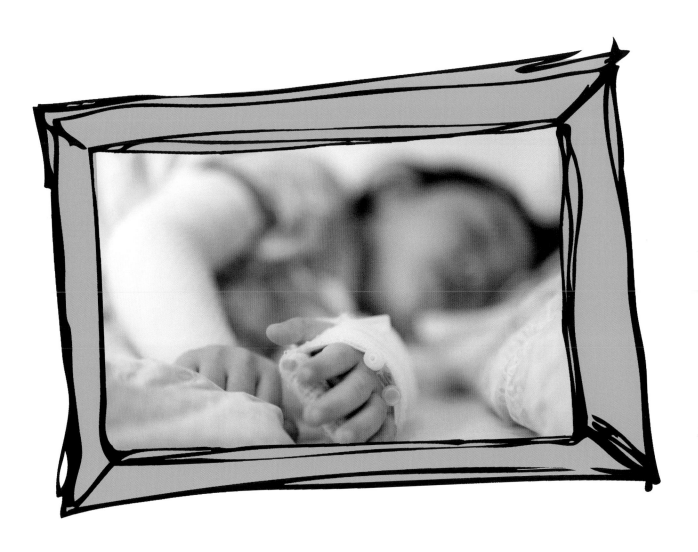

At school, I was different. Walking got hard. I used a wheelchair.

Who or what helps you?

It got harder to breathe. A machine helped. I studied disability. I was a **researcher**.

People like me weren't in movies. We weren't in shows. I wanted to change that.

I became an **activist**. I worked with President Barack Obama.

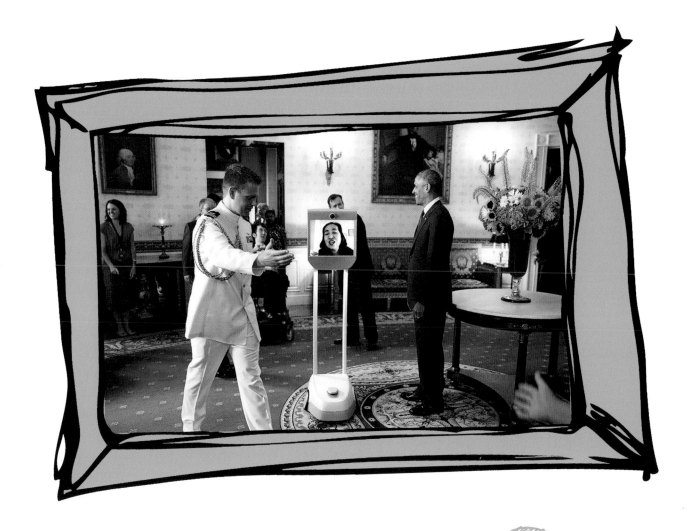

What is important to you?

I started a group. It is called the Disability **Visibility** Project. We share our stories.

Alice Wong Interview

I write. I speak out. I help the disability community grow.
I help it get strong.

No one should feel bad about who they are. I am proud of who I am!

What would you like to ask me?

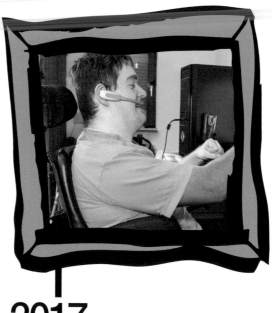

2017

1970

↑
Born
1974

2019

2070

glossary

activist (ACK-tuh-vist) someone who works to make things better for themselves or others, such as helping pass laws

disability (dis-uh-BIL-uh-tee) a difference in the way someone looks, moves around, or understands

researcher (REE-serch-er) someone who studies something carefully

visibility (viz-uh-BIL-uh-tee) amount something can be seen

index

Fred Rogers

Published in the United States of America by Cherry Lake Publishing Group
Ann Arbor, Michigan
www.cherrylakepublishing.com

Reading Adviser: Marla Conn, MS Ed., Literacy specialist, Read-Ability, Inc.
Book Designer: Jennifer Wahi
Illustrator: Jeff Bane

Photo Credits: ©Ohnoitsjamie/Wikimedia, 5; ©Rollins College Archives/resource ID studentmusicguild, 7; ©mike mols/shutterstock, 9, 22; ©Public Domain/Cowles Communications, Inc/Wikimedia, 11; ©Jer123/shutterstock, 13, 23; ©Monkey Business Images/shutterstock, 15; ©Craig At The Capitol/shutterstock, 17; ©National Archives Catalog/Photo by Paul Morse/ARC 7431400, 19; ©Public Domain/Photo by Terry Arthur/Wikimedia, 21; Jeff Bane, Cover, 1, 6, 14, 18

Cherry Lake Press is an imprint of Cherry Lake Publishing Group.

Library of Congress Cataloging-in-Publication Data

Names: Pincus, Meeg, author. | Bane, Jeff, 1957- illustrator.
Title: Fred Rogers / Meeg Pincus ; illustrated by Jeff Bane.
Description: Ann Arbor, Michigan : Cherry Lake Publishing, 2021. | Series: My itty-bitty bio | Includes index. | Audience: Grades K-1 | Summary: "The My Itty-Bitty Bio series are biographies for the earliest readers. This book examines the life of Fred Rogers, the man behind "Mister Rogers' Neighborhood," in a simple, age-appropriate way that will help young readers develop word recognition and reading skills. Includes a table of contents, author biography, timeline, glossary, index, and other informative backmatter"-- Provided by publisher.
Identifiers: LCCN 2020035933 (print) | LCCN 2020035934 (ebook) | ISBN 9781534179912 (hardcover) | ISBN 9781534181625 (paperback) | ISBN 9781534180925 (pdf) | ISBN 9781534182639 (ebook)
Subjects: LCSH: Rogers, Fred--Juvenile literature. | Television personalities--United States--Biography--Juvenile literature.
Classification: LCC PN1992.4.R56 P56 2021 (print) | LCC PN1992.4.R56 (ebook) | DDC 791.4502/8092 [B]--dc23
LC record available at https://lccn.loc.gov/2020035933
LC ebook record available at https://lccn.loc.gov/2020035934

Printed in the United States of America
Corporate Graphics

About the author: Meeg Pincus has been a writer, editor, and educator for 25 years. She loves to write inspiring stories for kids about people, animals, and our planet. She lives near San Diego, California, where she enjoys the beach, reading, singing, and her family.

About the illustrator: Jeff Bane and his two business partners own a studio along the American River in Folsom, California, home of the 1849 Gold Rush. When Jeff's not sketching or illustrating for clients, he's either swimming or kayaking in the river to relax.

I was born in Pennsylvania. It was 1928. My parents **adopted** my sister when I was 11.

I loved piano and puppets. I went to school to study music.

I watched my first television show when I was 20. It **inspired** me to work in television. I wanted to bring good shows to children.

What inspires you?

I married and had two sons.
I became a **minister**.

I started my own television show, *Mister Rogers' Neighborhood*. I used puppets. I wrote songs. My mom made me sweaters. I wore them on television.

I listened to children. I talked about feelings.

How does it feel when someone listens to you?

I spoke to **Congress** to save **public television**. I wanted television shows that **support** children.

17

My show ran for 33 years.
I was an **advocate** for
children. I won many awards.

I died in 2003. But my message of caring for others continues today.

What would you like to ask me?

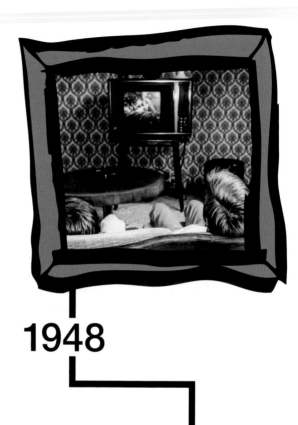

1948

1920

Born
1928

1966

2020

↑
Died
2003

glossary

adopted (uh-DAHPT-id) to bring a person into your family

advocate (AD-vuh-kit) a person who stands up for another

Congress (KAHNG-gris) the lawmaking body of the United States

inspired (in-SPIRED) to be filled with a feeling or an idea

minister (MIN-ih-stur) a person whose job involves leading church services

public television (PUHB-lik TEL-uh-vizh-uhn) television that has many educational programs and receives some funding from the government and citizens

support (suh-PORT) to provide help, money, or comfort

index